# SO TO SPEAK

# SO TO SPEAK

## Terrance Hayes

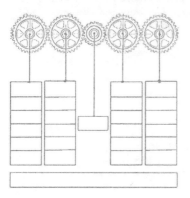

PENGUIN POETS

**PENGUIN BOOKS**
An imprint of Penguin Random House LLC
penguinrandomhouse.com

Pages 89–90 constitute an extension of this copyright page.

All art by Terrance Hayes.

LIBRARY OF CONGRESS CATALOGING-IN-PUBLICATION DATA
Names: Hayes, Terrance, author.
Title: So to speak / Terrance Hayes.
Description: [New York] : Penguin Books, [2023] | Series: Penguin poets
Identifiers: LCCN 2022055375 (print) | LCCN 2022055376 (ebook) |
ISBN 9780143137726 (paperback) | ISBN 9780593511848 (ebook)
Subjects: LCGFT: Poetry.
Classification: LCC PS3558.A8378 S6 2023 (print) |
LCC PS3558.A8378 (ebook) | DDC 811/.54—dc23/eng/20221115
LC record available at https://lccn.loc.gov/2022055375
LC ebook record available at https://lccn.loc.gov/2022055376

Printed in the United States of America
2nd Printing

Set in Berling Std
Designed by Sabrina Bowers

*for Ua & Aaron*
*& for my students*

# CONTENTS

"—a thing like me . . ."

*Brigit Pegeen Kelly, "Closing Time; Iskandariya"*

# SO TO SPEAK

# AMERICAN SONNET FOR THE NEW YEAR

Things got terribly ugly incredibly quickly
Things got ugly embarrassingly quickly
actually Things got ugly unbelievably quickly
honestly Things got ugly seemingly infrequently
initially Things got ugly ironically usually
awfully carefully Things got ugly unsuccessfully
occasionally Things got ugly mostly painstakingly
quietly seemingly Things got ugly beautifully
infrequently Things got ugly sadly especially
frequently unfortunately Things got ugly
increasingly obviously Things got ugly suddenly
embarrassingly forcefully Things got really ugly
regularly truly quickly Things got really incredibly
ugly Things will get less ugly inevitably hopefully

# WATCH YOUR MOUTH

# PSEUDACRIS CRUCIFER

*For Aaron*

The father begins to make the sound a tree frog makes
When he comes with his son & daughter to a pail
Of tree frogs for sale in a Deep South flea market
Just before the last blood of dusk.
A tree frog is called a tree frog because it chirps
Like a bird in a tree, he tells his daughter
While her little brother, barely four years old,
Busies himself like a small blues piper
With a brand-new birthday harmonica.
A single tree frog can sound like a sleigh bell,
The father says. Several can sound like a choir
Of crickets. Once in high school as I dissected
A frog, the frog opened its eyes to judge
Its deconstruction, its disassembly,
My scooping & poking at its soul.
And the little girl's eyes go wide as a tree frog's eyes.
Some call it "the spring peeper." In Latin
It's called *Pseudacris crucifer*. False locusts,
Toads with falsettos, their chimes issuing below
The low leaves & petals. The harmonica playing
Is so otherworldly, the boy blows with his eyes closed.
Some tree frog species spend most every day underground.
They don't know what sunlight does at dusk.
They are nocturnal insectivores. No bigger than
A green thumb, they are the first frogs to call
In the spring. They may sound like crickets
Only because they eat so many crickets.
Tree frogs mostly sound like birds.
The tree frog overcomes its fear of birds by singing.
The harmonica playing is so bewitching,
The boy gathers a crowd in a flea market
In the Deep South. A bird may eat a tree frog.
A fox may eat the bird. A wolf may eat the fox.

And the wolf, then, may carry varieties of music
And cunning in its belly as it roams the countryside.
A wolf hungers because it cannot feel the good
In its body. The people clap & gather round
With fangs & smiles. The father lifts the son
To his shoulders so the boy's harmonics hover
Over varieties of affections, varieties of bodies
With their backs to a firmament burning & opening.
You can find damn near anything in a flea market:
Pets, weapons, flags, farm-fresh as well as farm-spoiled
Fruits & vegetables, varieties of old wardrobes,
A rusty old tin box with old postcards & old photos
Of lynchings dusted in the rust of the box.
You can feel it on the tips of your fingers,
This rust, which is almost as brown as the father
And the boy on his shoulders & the girl making
The sound a tree frog makes in a flea market
In the Deep South before the last blood of dusk,
Just before the last blood of dusk. Just before the dusk.

# STRANGE AS THE RULES OF GRAMMAR

Ladies & Gentlemen put your hands together
for Kareem Abdul-Jabbar's beautifully iambic name

Do not think of all the tall in him
squeezing into a stall at the mall as strange

Some days his father whispered to himself
Someday that boy's going to change his name

I ran away from home as soon as I had a chance
when I was four or five in the Carolinas

Certain words never used to cross my mind
A god who claims to be on the side of good

but remains hidden is strange as the rules of grammar
The mouth fills with mouthfuls of grammar

Strange as the flowers a lost child finds
in the woods & consumes

Strange as that "that!" a toddler cries in public
when something shiny appears

a candy hard as a ruby wrapped in plastic
a lonely coin blinking in the grass

or at the bottom of a fountain
within the toddler's grasp

The first time my parents left me alone
with a babysitter I ran away before noon

They spent hours looking for me
before going home to find I had been

waiting on the porch the whole day
they say

You too may recall a story
so old you never thought to mention it to anybody

Strange as the first wound you ever received
The scar so old others must tell you how it was made

# GEORGE FLOYD

You can be a bother who dyes
his hair Dennis Rodman blue
in the face of the man kneeling in blue
in the face the music of his wrist-
watch your mouth is little more
than a door being knocked
out of the ring of fire around
the afternoon came evening's bell
of the ball & chain around the neck
of the unarmed brother ground down
to gunpowder dirt can be inhaled
like a puff the magic bullet point
of transformation both kills & fires
the life of the party like it's 1999 bottles
of beer on the wall street people
who sleep in the streets do not sleep
without counting yourself lucky
rabbit's foot of the mountain
lion do not sleep without
making your bed of the river
boat gambling there will be
no stormy weather on the water
bored to death any means of killing
time is on your side of the bed
of the truck transporting Emmett
till the break of day Emmett till
the river runs dry your face
the music of the spheres
Emmett till the end of time

# FOLK STONE

In my next life      let me be      dear black bird
Born with a foot      on the ass      of all assholes

None of them will remember me
More startled than starlight or starling last year hidden

In the bushes      beside a river      running down the valley
In my next life      let me be      dear black bear

Strong enough to pull my childish true enemy
From the dark village      down the street

Where Monk's imitators play      the same nonlinear blues
I spend the lonely evenings playing

Force him to comb the underworld      for the book
I left beside a girl      on a subway

Covered in footnotes      & illegible handwriting
Dream versus Sincerity      Thinking versus Feeling

Machine versus Engine      Shade versus Shadow
The people who come after you      versus the people behind you

Anything versus Everything      Poem versus Piano
If I live to be a four-year-old      black girl      again

My sky-black dress  will never be as black      as my afro
If I live to be a ten-year-old      shotgun      again

Black as an anvil      full of buckshot      raise me      with my mother
In the most southern      & southernmost      of the Carolinas

Force our enemies to gather      all the stones in a beautiful meadow
While singing      strange godly gospels      to pass the time

# AMERICAN SONNET FOR *INNERVISIONS*

When James Baldwin & Audre Lorde each lend
Stevie Wonder an eyeball, he immediately contends
With gravity, falling either to his knees or flat on
His luminous face. I've heard various versions
Of the story. In this one Audre Lorde dons
Immaculate French loafers, turtlenecked ball gown,
And afro halo. An eye-sized ruby glimmers on
A pinkie ring that's a hair too big for Jimmy Baldwin's
Pinkie. He's blue with beauty. They're accustomed
To being followed, but now, the eye-patch twins
Will be especially scary to white people. Looking upon
Them, Stevie Wonder's head purples with plural visions
Of blackness, gavels, grapples, purrs, pens. Odds are ten
To one God also prefers to be referred to as They & Them.

# THE PRINCE OF CLEVELAND

I realize it is time to complete the poem
presenting reasons to visit Cleveland,
but I don't think I will be able to do so
until I am actually sitting in Cleveland
writing about the view from my hotel
window in a part of the city the city intends
to gentrify. The bricks of the empty
newly constructed office building
have been replaced with less historical bricks.
They have just about finished the work,
the men who painted the bricks a colonial
white & have left fluorescent lights buzzing
all night on the floors to discourage
squatters like the brother I see on the street
outside the building belted in what is either
a black leather jacket or black plastic trash bag
belting "Purple Rain" poorly, but earnestly.
He likely sings throughout the day for money
and tourists seeking the Rock & Roll Hall of Fame
where they will find a mural of Prince
but no Prince made of wax. Hotel windows
are locked not for fear of suicides,
but because open windows encourage smoking.
Outside, the voice of the Prince of Cleveland
is high as fire. I can tell he smokes.
He favors my uncle around the eyes.
Would you like to know your future? he asks
when I find myself smoking next to him.
He has made a lucrative fortune-telling
business with little more than a lawn chair,
a card table & playing cards. I decline.
One of the doors of the office building
is unlocked. Drop cloths, buckets,
trash bags. One of those old boom boxes

you never see anymore. My uncle used
to have one. It was in his bedroom
I first saw a Prince record, though I didn't know
it was Prince at the time. I thought it was
a mustached & hairy woman on a horse.
I can still hear my host coughing & singing
a few floors below on the other side
of the office building windows & the cry
of a siren crossing the city. You don't look up
when I look across the boulevard into the room
of your hotel, but I know you know I'm here.

## HOMAGE TO GERTRUDE BADU

If your momma was fine as half a bottle of honey wine,
Or your daddy cool as a coin tossed in a wishing well,
Well, yeah she might compliment your style,

But more often than not her eyeglasses was tuned
To whatever she was illegally spray-painting on the war streets.

If Clay & Lula from Amiri Baraka's 1964 play *Dutchman*
Had a baby—I mean if Lula & the white folks hadn't killed

Brother Clay—what do I suppose would have been the first
And middle name of their baby? This is what she asked
Before signing my yearbook so no telling what she felt for me.

Her shoes? I think they called them moon or maybe miner's boots.
Once when she stooped to blow smoke into the mouth
Of a neighbor's pit bull, I saw the glitter on her G-string.

Her & the pigtailed cashier from the corner store
Stole the preacher's two-pound Bible.
She spoke nothing but verbs & sighs to priests.

Her & a girl with a head of freckles broke into the Mickey D,
The Joann Fabric, the back rub parlor & left the goods
On the lawn of our retired high school principal.

You know what you call someone who wins by cheating?
She asked me later that day: A winner.
No one lives in adult movies, she used to say.

If I recited all the laws of the Gnostics,
She promised to kiss me in some mysterious way
On some even more mysterious part of my longing.

She told me *trombone* was always the word of the day.
Also: Anytime one finds oneself facing oneself in a mirror
One must say to the mirror, "You don't know shit about me."
She used to say you can't be free trapped in a body.

## DIY SESTINA:
## WHAT DOES THE PIECE REMIND YOU OF?

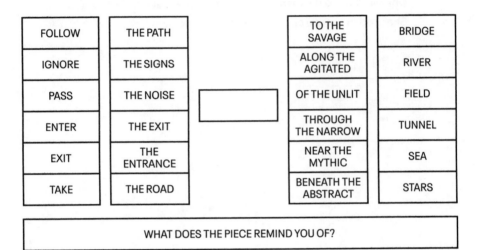

| | | | |
|---|---|---|---|
| FOLLOW | THE PATH | TO THE SAVAGE | BRIDGE |
| IGNORE | THE SIGNS | ALONG THE AGITATED | RIVER |
| PASS | THE NOISE | OF THE UNLIT | FIELD |
| ENTER | THE EXIT | THROUGH THE NARROW | TUNNEL |
| EXIT | THE ENTRANCE | NEAR THE MYTHIC | SEA |
| TAKE | THE ROAD | BENEATH THE ABSTRACT | STARS |

WHAT DOES THE PIECE REMIND YOU OF?

\* \* \*

### [*THE NEGRO IN AN AFRICAN SETTING,* BY AARON DOUGLAS, 1934]

Take the hazy overlook toward the Negroes in the stars.
Stay on the overlook toward the mouth of the river.
Pass the Negroes parked in the dark & hiding in the field.
Take River Styx Boulevard to the pyramid, go through the tunnel.
Pass through an agitated rain forest & get on the ramp to the bridge
After several hours on the bridge, take the exit to the sea.

### [*ICARUS,* BY HENRI MATISSE, 1947]

Take the unlit shape of one of the blacks you see
In the scene & make a Henri Matisse collage of six yellow stars.
Stencil the unlit figure on all the crosswalk signs for drivers.
Hello to the Negroes parked in the dark & hiding in the field.
Follow the Matisse hiding in Hank Willis Thomas with tunnel
Vision. After the last crosswalk sign, take the next bridge.

## [*MECKLENBURG AUTUMN: HEAT LIGHTNING EASTWARD*, BY ROMARE BEARDEN, 1983]

Do not enter the river. Relax on a quilt on the bank with your bride.
Leave the door of your gray house open for all to see.
Take eight-hour siestas whether the sky fills with lightning or stars.
Follow the eyes of your bride watching trouble rise in the river.
Take time admiring how good your guitar makes you feel
Passing a hand over its strings as your bride hums its tune.

## [*GOING HOME*, BY JACOB LAWRENCE, 1946]

Head along the river until you come to the long railroad tunnel
Through the mountain, take the second left after the bridge.
Follow the signs through towns no one built to withstand a siege
Of poverty or weather. Employ tunnel vision amid the stares
Should you pause for rest. Do not enter the river.
Hello to the Negroes resting on the train riding over the field.

## [*FACE DOWN*, BY MARTIN PURYEAR, 2008]

Head downhill into the valley avoiding where floodwaters fill
The lanes. Every hole in the ground is an unfinished tunnel.
Take a shovel for burying seeds & bodies beneath the bridge.
Take just the front half of your face & say what you see
When you lower it into a basin of river lit by lightning & stars.
Follow signs of the creatures who live at the edge of the river.

## [*HAYSTACKS*, BY HENRY OSSAWA TANNER, CA. 1930]

Stay on the overlook toward the mouth of the river.
Pass the Negroes parked in the dark & hiding in the field.
You can almost see *Face Down* in *Haystacks* if you use tunnel
Vision. Hello to the Negroes crossing a bridge.
Take the shape of one of the Negroes you see.
Take the overlook whether the sky fills with lightning or stars.

*  *  *

## ENVOY OF WILLIAM H. JOHNSON'S *NUDE*

When Precious Jackson, a middle-aged black woman
Whose personalized license plate simply read QUEEN,
Discovered William H. Johnson's *Nude*, ca. 1939, oil

On burlap, hanging in a museum recently, she underwent
What my mother described as an Octavia Butlering,
A temporal transfixion so fierce she excused herself

From her small tribe of Baptists up from South Carolina,
Following a nervous tour guide around a museum in DC.
Just before Aaron Douglas's *The Negro in an African*

*Setting* made my mother hallucinate something
She still refuses to share with me, she recalled Precious's
Melodramatic skedaddle. Jackson was found

Hyperventilating in a bathroom stall by my mother,
Who also happened to be her roommate on the road
And who knew Jackson suffered bouts of insomnia,

Half sleepwalking the halls of hotels nosing
The ice machines &/or eavesdropping on the room
Of Pastor Evans. When Precious gazed upon the nude

Black woman in William H. Johnson's 1939 painting
She swore she recalled the scene, him watching her watch
Him watch her looking at him fuss & mutter over the painting.

She started rocking & sweating, my mother said,
Like she was filled with the Holy Spirit, then
Precious said the light falling on her nipples that day

Was like the feel of Johnson's brush. His touch
Could turn burlap to silk. There was a tiny bit of wine
In a glass beside an emptied bottle just as in the painting,

But there was also a tiny bit of the nectar in the air
And on her lips. My mother told her
To wash her face & bring her tail on. The rest

Of the church members knew how to look
Without suffering a public vision.
*The Negro in an African Setting* is not quite like the Negro

Of Loïs Mailou Jones's *Africa* nor the Negro in Winold
Reiss's *African Phantasy* is all my mother will tell me
Of her own vision. My mother added,

Don't you know when that girl came to Elizabeth Catlett's
Wood sculpture of a black woman made of mahogany,
She claimed again she was there when Catlett carved it.

Except this time, she said, she was not the model,
She was the tree. She said she recalled living as the tree
Catlett was carving to reveal the precious body

Beneath the bark. When I asked "Like Michelangelo?"
My mother said, "No, like Pinocchio."
The word *mahogany* comes to us

From the West Indies by way of the enslaved
West Africans who hid its bark in their mouths
When they were seized. The wood is used in boats

Because of its resistance to rot, but it is also found
In the necks & bodies of guitars. One can see
How a black woman might see some of herself in the tree.

# AMERICAN SONNET FOR MY GRANDFATHER'S LOVE CHILD

You take a tree where all the blackbirds are sleeping,
Except for the one clapping its wings: that's the kind
Of woman who raised me. My mother changed her name
To daughter, then to sister, then back to mother again.
Three times, she parked outside her wretched father's house
Undertaking a melancholy kind of karaoke, she can't sing
Really, she's ashamed of her teeth, but she pretended
An emcee was saying *Give her a hand* when she finished.
I wasn't there, but I bet she jangled her car keys
As if she was offering a small girl a ride to the beach,
To the oceanside, to the water a girl becomes to survive
And the soft applause washing ashore when she retreats.
To love her I had to love the night curling up around me.
I woke up surprised whether she was coming or going.

## TAFFETA

I wanted to wear the Frederick Douglass T-shirt
because it's as close as I'll ever be to Frederick
Douglass. I wanted to appear revolutionary
and decorous entering the day like a needful star,
superb in love & logic. My mother often says
she's so happy she didn't kill me when she found out
she was pregnant. She's so glad she didn't give me
to the old woman who asked to adopt me.
When sweat weeps along the sides of my ribs
from the two great stains yellowing my shirt pits,
I'm like a man ashamed by his own tears.
I used to keep my arms clamped at my sides
the hot days of my adolescence in South Carolina.
The last time I visited, my mother told me how,
when her handyman gave the waitress
sweating before them a ten-dollar tip, the waitress
gave him in return the keys to the apartment
she lived in with her delicate twenty-year-old son.
He whined, "Why, Mamma?" exactly like a daughter
anticipating the heartache the mother was courting.
"Why would you let somebody you barely know
into our house?" That boy used to turn all the heads
in town, my mother told me, & though he was fatter now
because of the drugs he took with a mind to change
himself into a woman, he was still easily mistaken
for a girl in a sundress with his milkless breasts,
and gooseflesh swaddling his belly & biceps.
Two months later the handyman & the waitress
broke up. He was not even that handy, really,
he was just out of work & hired by my mother
to repair some leak or shamble, & because
she did not pay him much, sometimes she'd take
him to lunch. I sweat imagining his fingers sliding
over a woman whose mouth opened

as if she were praying or giving birth. Taffeta
is the kind of cloth that makes a sound
when you touch it. It sounds like flowers
being painted on a dress. It falls in a crush
by the bed & the tongue folds around
a lonely center & because of it,
your son changes his name to Taffeta
when he becomes female. Nature's favorite color
is green. Taffeta's dress is covered in flowers.
At sixteen I wore my mother's dress to school
and stood on a stage with three other boys
in lipstick lip-synching to the Mary Jane Girls.
I loved the feel of cloth folding around
my movement. That dress still hangs somewhere
waiting to be worn, its sheen & she-ness
shameless & sweat-stained. There's a yearbook
photo to prove I wore it but it's true
a photograph, especially when it's an image
of flesh, grows, over time, more & more
strange. You are not you for long.
I am not trying to change the world,
I am trying to change myself
so that the world will seem changed.

# AMERICAN SONNET STARRING OCTAVIA BUTLER I

In Julie Dash's *Octavia Butler* the director washes Octavia's
Monumental feet & toenails in buckets of government water
When there are no seas or rivers handy. It takes too long
Awaiting God's drizzle though there are open barrels outside
The camera's frame in the scene where Butler lies outdoors
Letting her entire mouth fill with tap water, then spitting the water
Into the air blessed & better after the taste of her speech.
If you don't see suffering's potential as art, will it remain suffering?
When Butler tells Dash she's dreamed of storms all week,
Dash asks to film the dreams. The camera watches Butler sleep
A full moon humming something in the same baritone she uses
When she speaks. Of course, Octavia Butler stars in *Octavia Butler*.
She buys blouses with patterns of leaves & flowers in the off-hours
And listens to the young hotel desk clerk worry about precipitous weather.

# ARS POETICA WITH BACON

Fortunately, the family, anxious about its diminishing
food supply, encountered a small, possibly hostile pig
along the way. The daughter happened upon it first
pushing its scuffed snout against something hidden
at the base of a thornbush: a blood-covered egg, maybe,
or a small rubber ball exactly like the sort that snapped
from the paddle my mother used to beat me with
when I let her down. At the time the father & mother
were tangled in some immemorial dispute about cause
and effect: who'd harmed whom first, how jealousy
did not, in fact, begin as jealousy, but as desperation.
When the daughter called out to them, they turned
to see her lift the pig, it was no heavier than an orphan,
from the bushes & then set it down in their path.
They waited to see whether the pig might idle forward
with them until they made camp or wander back toward
the home they'd abandoned to war. Night, enclosed
in small drops of rain, began to fall upon them.
*Consequence* is the word that splintered my mind.
Walking a path in the dark is about something
the way a family is about something. Like the pig,
I too wanted to reach through the thorns for the egg
or ball, believing it was a symbol of things to come.
I wanted to roll it in my palm like the head
of a small redbird until it sang to me. I wanted
to know how my mother passed her days having
never touched her husband's asshole, for example.
Which parts of your body have never been touched?
I wanted to ask. I'd been hired to lead the family
from danger to a territory full of more seeds than bullets,
but truth was, in the darkness there was no telling
what was rooting in the soil. Plots of complete silence,
romantics posing in a field bludgeoned by shame.
The heart, biologically speaking, is ugly as it pumps

its passion & fear down the veins. Which is to say,
starting out we have no wounds to speak of
beyond the ways our parents expressed their love.
We were never sure what the pig was after or whether
it was, in fact, not a pig, but some single-minded soul
hunger turned into a pig, some devil worthy of mercy.
Without giving away the enigmatic ending, I will say
when we swallowed the flesh, our eyes were closed.

# WATCH YOUR STEP: THE KAFKA VIRUS

# AN EXTENDED PUBLIC SERVICE ANNOUNCEMENT

*April 2020*

Mark your calendars now, Brothers & Sisters,
For end-of-the-year Watch Night services in the area.
Spend twilight to midnight in a house with a pulpit
And pews of atmospheric fellowship.

If you are lost as a child's muddy shoe beside
An anxious river, if water gathers beneath your nails
When you touch it, get free of the twisted root.
Some night it may be Freedom's Eve again.

You may find yourself in a room somewhere
In the near past or distant future awaiting Lincoln's
Decree. Upon the proclamation, two contests
Of resistance may ensue like two troubled storms

Making a violent path to the sea. You may dress
Like a worshipper in the bowels of a warship
Made of money & forest parts. You may
Quench your thirst with the rain on your lashes.

You may dress like the woman who scours
The schoolhouse until it is clean enough for church.
The room may have been built according
To the architecture of farmers & teachers

Dressed as slaves. (After several hours working
For the nothings of enslavers black people
Raised the scaffolding of holy shelters in the dark.)
Someone may have slaughtered & prepared the cow

That provided the hide for the preacher's Bible.
Someone may have smuggled raw cotton from the field
And later worked it until it was useful cloth.
The cross may be made of a blacksmith's scraps,

A master carpenter's timber, or two bound branches
With a few almost imperceptible buds opening
Along the bark. You may be asked to wash the hands
Of an enemy. You may begin the night with your fists

In knots of strong opposition & end it
With your palms fanning your awe in woozy light.
You may hear tales of the hour the state upgraded
Black folk from property to slightly more free.

You may fall in love with a good listener,
Find food & drink in the cafeteria,
A visitor, such as yourself, sequestered an entire year
In America, may find your name turns to music

When spoken on Watch Night. If you feel like a tourist
In a war-torn country, come figure it out with us.
Area churches welcome you to service. Mother
Emanuel, New Horizons, Macedonia, Bridge of Life,

Heaven's Door, visitors, welcomed to churches featuring
Street names & whereabouts, the names of saints,
Apostles, angels, kings, & servants, names featuring
Charity, Restoration, Faith. First African is not far

From Second African, the Chapel of Redemption is between
The House of Conviction & the Temple of Forgiveness,
There's a great organist at the Shepherd's Tabernacle,
The Eighth Avenue Church of Eve's Destiny is across the street

From the Eighth Avenue Church of Adam's Redemption.
One-hundred-year-old twins sing at the Olive Branch
House of Holiness in Christ. The list of services
Is not exhaustive. Cancellation never happens.

This is a public service announcement.
Mark your calendars. Tomorrow loves you.
Join us or contact us & we will spread the word
If your place of worship has Watch Night plans.

# AMERICAN SONNET FOR FIRE & LIGHTNING

By age two, gentleman toddler Mandela was known
From mountain to valley for his stellar storytelling skills.
They sat him directly on podiums or on church pulpits
Or let him stand on wobbly tables in markets
And schoolhouses, falling a few times, without injury.
Often he told variations of a tale where blind men
Discuss the varieties of light. Sometimes, because he was
Still a baby, he spit up a substance the blue
In certain shades of honey. In fact, years later,
If he coughed while telling prisoners & prison guards
Bedtime tales, they say his jaws flashed a color somewhere
Between fire & lightning. He'd say, "Excuse me," kind
Even at two years old, then resume his supernatural story-
Telling. Folks far & wide would go home laughing & crying.

# DO NOT PUT YOUR HEAD UNDER YOUR ARM

*An Analogue PechaKucha, 2020*

¯\_(ツ)_/¯
It appears I will never be remembered
as a great singer nor extravagant eater.
Either I am standing or I am dreaming.
Or I am standing near the mouth of a theater.

¯\_(:-|)_/¯
One early & deeply progressive symptom
of the Kafka Virus: a stream of movies seeps
into the shell of the infected individual's sleeping.
Dream factors greatly in the disease.

¯\_('-')_/¯
I accept I may never get over the ways my mother
loved me poorly. She is close to God in me.
On a planet in a day without surefire gods
& mythologies, there is the religion of family.

¯\_(--)_/¯
Inside the stream of Whitney Houston's
voice, Dionne Warwick warns,
"You're gonna need me one
day. You're gonna want me back in your arms."

¯\_(:-|)_/¯
There are no ugly people, only expressions
of ugliness, when the mouth is set
this way or that. It's best to think of time
the way a miser thinks of money.

¯\\_(' ')_/¯

Matisse liked to have the nude near to see her,
but Picasso liked to close his eyes upon her.
What I remember of 1987 is mostly what I remember
of '88 except with different deaths & births.

¯\\_(:-|)_/¯

If you watch Hitchcock's *Vertigo*
the other way round, you may notice
inside the movie is a whole other movie
told from the point of view of the young lady.

¯\\_(--)_/¯

Each new pair of glasses assures things
never look the same, but several glasses
of liquor can create the same feeling.
Balance the morass & the molasses of jackasses.

¯\\_('-')_/¯

Even where I doubt the presence of God
I am awed by the scale of creation.
Any science suggesting all that happens
is coincidence, is nonsense.

¯\\_('.')_/¯

"Intrepidation." "Misfortunate." "Ya-licious."
"Holy smoked turkey." "Attack of the third dimension."
I continue to half believe a fourth *s*
resides somewhere inside the word *obsession*.

¯\\_(:-|)_/¯

Clap for a low back country road
like a tree talking below a constellation.
A low back river talking twilight
with the leaves clapping below a constellation.

¯\_('')_/¯

Often right after taking a photo you immediately
crop or color the image so it seems
the doctored thing is the memory.
I'm not saying you have to lie to dream.

¯\_(:-|)_/¯

I stream the sequel to a terrible disaster
movie where the protagonist searches for a lover
with the support of characters who meet catastrophe
helping the main character.

¯\_('-')_/¯

The gun is lowered but then a toe
or two in the boot is shot & when the shoe
comes off, there's a hole a grandchild or two
a generation or two later can put a finger through.

¯\_(:-|)_/¯

Before the sleeping dream,
we are told to keep nickels in the glasses
of wine by our beds. The virus seems
to have some relationship to cash.

¯\_('')_/¯

Clap for *Tetris*, the video game
that teaches you the most geometry for life.
Stacks of boxes of books, closets of hangers
and monster angels and historical fabrics.

¯\_('-')_/¯

I was struck by the sky of my South
Carolina. It made my mouth ache.
I was old by the time I heard the prophet
Isaiah used to preach naked.

¯\_(:-|)_/¯
Ghost, the loss that broke you was so
ubiquitous, I failed to see it lingering in the ether
like the misspelled affections that go
undetected by both letter writer & letter reader.

¯\_(--)_/¯
Often I confuse *Vivamus, moriendum est,*
which means "Let us live, for we must die,"
with *Bibamus, moriendum est,* which means "Let
us drink, for we must die."

¯\_(:-|)_/¯
Isamu Noguchi sculpted the marrow
of a black stone into bamboo & planted husks
of live bamboo shoots to guard it. I know
this ragged clock waits to be clogged with dust.

## A GHAZALLED SENTENCE AFTER "MY PEOPLE . . . HOLD ON," BY EDDIE KENDRICKS, AND THE NEGRO ACT OF 1740

WHEREIN, a particular people
are allowed to make slaves of people

after the 1739 revolt where people convinced
tools useful in implementing their people's

freedom had been stolen from them pursued
people to a river shallow enough for people

to cross on horseback & some of the people leapt
into the river kicking their legs like people

on the riverbank kicking the legs of the horses
& the people on the horses while some people

managed to briefly evade retrieval
by people who could not see that people

they pursued could not be retrieved,
People,

because your body belongs to you,
& certainly not to the kind of people

who devised laws to make properties
of people after the people

at the river were captured, their heads
put on stakes along the road & people

who briefly eluded pursuit before
being recouped or returned to people

so afraid of working for themselves
they made it illegal for other people

to work for themselves, grow their own food,
congregate & educate their own people,

without say-so of the kind of people who come
after people pursuing freedom for their people

while pursing freedom for the people
who come after their people.

# MAPS OF STATES

*May 2020*

A map indicating the state of the union may
Yield the statues, static & statutes of grave
White men, while a map indicating disrepair may
Yield colorful groundbreakers uprooting graves.

A map indicating the state of your affairs may
Include only the business of your accountant.
If you can steer clear of laissez-faire, do. You may
Be sorry if you take the wrong road down the mountain.

A map indicating states of arousal may
Also be a map few people find useful
Though the people who feel this way may
Also be people in a state of denial.

A map indicating a state of inertia may
Be indistinguishable from a map
Indicating a state of flux. The route may
Lead you in circles around the map.

A map indicating a state-of-the-art May-
Bach may feature what could be mistaken
For peace signs or tiny wheels making
Their way across a larger map that may

Indicate a state of grace under fire or may
Indicate a state of emergency exit, a route
Which may divide at forks in the road or may
Multiply at crossroads leading you out

Into a light so bright & constant you may
Have to wear a cap & shades indoors
Like brothers who know as much about May-
Bachs as Bach pursuing cultural studies or

The mother tongue of New York, they may
Wear peace signs on their shoulders
Traveling states of aggression that may
Actually be states of preservation or

Distress. A map indicating a state of war may
Actually be a map indicating a state
Of weariness. Let your eyes fall where they may
On the map indicating your state.

You may wander the states of wonder indicated
By the many unmarked areas along the map.
Almost anything you see is a map in some way.
Let your eyes fall where they may on the maps.

# MUSCULAR FANTASY

*October 2020*

I was thinking about that museum
with just the one painted stamp people
pay big money to stare at minimum
an hour at a time by a painter of people

who have been old for a very long time.
Sarah Beth Bess of Paducah, Old Walter Thom
outside Parris Island, the most senior clients
of most of the low-country senior homes.

There used to be a country where no sad
songs were allowed out loud because
making the king blue was outlawed.
The girl falling down the well sang without pause

as she fell. People described it as gospel.
The boy in the well sang as well as a small bell
& the people said it sounded like babble.
Rising in lifelike detail from the middle

of the stamp-sized painting is an ornate mountain.
My people moved further south to the beaches
instead of moving north after Reconstruction.
"Blessed," my father said when I asked if he'd

rather be blessed or lucky. Soda in a can taste better
than soda in a bottle but beer in a bottle
taste better than beer in a can. It's better
plus less stressful to think the best of people.

The worst thing about scared people
is they go around scaring other people.

Who you are with your mamma, People,
is not who you are with other people.

The color of my mother's thumbs-up emoji
is unchanged either because she's not estranged
by such things or because she doesn't know
the shade of her thumb can be changed.

The painter can be seen painting a small
painting through the window of a modestly
decorated cabin on the mountain. With all
the people who clap when some mostly

vengeful violence happens in the scene,
those who do not clap may feel no other people
are not clapping. I hear you. It seems
reasonable to stare at a painting for at least

as long as it takes the painter to make it
& also reasonable to stare for approximately
as long as it takes the sun to rise & set.
I told my father being blessed was vaguely

more dependent on the whims of God.
I'd rather be lucky. The girl in the well
was put there in the name of a god
created by farming people. The boy fell.

# AMERICAN SONNET FOR MY PAST AND FUTURE ASSASSIN

When Aretha & Nina sang "Mary, Don't You Weep"
Into the same mic, levitating on stage, the future dictator,
Age six or eight, ward of a black maid for a Sunday, was asleep.
(We pine for a timeline wherein he remained awake.)
The tiny yellow flowers, yellow sparks & yellow jackets
Swarming out of the mouths of the divas in this dazzling,
Undocumented happening distracted no one attached
To their singing. No one saw when one woman took
The other by the hand or what appeared between them
When they let go. Some guess a celestial rope or roadway,
Or the disembodied robe of Lazarus, or one of them held
The head & the other the tail of the snake being returned
To the garden as if nothing could be holier than forgiving
Him. In any case, the future dictator was not awake.

# ILLUSTRATED OCTAVIA BUTLER DO-IT-YOURSELF SESTINA

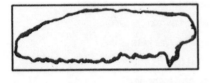

| | | | | | |
|---|---|---|---|---|---|
| GIVEN | THE LIGHT | | YOUR | HANDS |
| FORBIDDEN | THE EVENING | | MY | EYES |
| SEEKING | THE LANGUAGE | INSIDE | A FAMILY'S | MOUTH |
| FINDING | THE SPIRIT | | AN ENEMY'S | NOSE |
| AFTER | THE EARTH | | A STRANGER'S | ARMS |
| ROOTING | THE SEED | | A LOVER'S | TOES |

## STANZA 1

## STANZA 2

## STANZA 3

**STANZA 4**

**STANZA 5**

**STANZA 6**

**STANZA 7 ENVOY**

# THINGS SEEN RIGHT & LEFT WITHOUT GLASSES

*August 2020*

Sometimes I feel like a motherless town
full of fathers who get custody of their sons
in the divorce, a town of hotels & campers
and men & boys who speak as strangers

but feel the blood they share.
I remember the policeman arrested the child
after hitting him so hard, his face caved
in the nightmare & the sound woke me.

My cry can be heard if you lay an ear
to my Adam's apple, named so as proof
it was Adam that tried to swallow
where Eve only tried to bite the fruit.

Everything said & unsaid issues from us
like a humming, like honey clogging the pipes
with sweetness. Sometimes I feel like dancing.
We gonna dance the night away.

Sometimes I feel like somebody's watching me.
Sometimes I feel like I got to run away.
Sometimes I feel like the child whose disfigured
expression was placed in a fishbowl.

Why would anyone ever truly want to relax?
Where I'm from everybody fights everybody
to get to truly know them. I plan to change
my mind according to intuition's Venn diagram

of the people who know the truth overlapping
with people who don't know the truth

overlapping with people who know the truth
but lie about it overlapping with people

who don't know the truth but think they do.
We're in the colorful gray between up & down.
Have mercy, I hear you say. It may not be
right or wrong. It may not be true or false.

Sometimes I feel like someone who parks
with the headlights facing the road.
Sometimes I feel like someone who parks
with the headlights facing the house.

Not so much the tongue as its negotiation
with the throat & teeth. Not so much a muscle
as a space for mediating the bite & swallow.
As if the spine is a hollowed bony pole with teeth

around a throat attached to the gastrointestinal tract
attached to the anus. Sometimes I feel like Alice
proves nothing's wrong with a rabbit hole.
There must be a place to process what is taken in

and what is released. Throw your hands in the air
and wave like you're changing a light bulb.
Remember the first time you stayed up past midnight
like someone who was almost a know-it-all?

# AMERICAN SONNET & GOLDEN SHOVEL FOR THE TREE OF LIBERTY

Regarding my meditations & notes on *the*
Constitution constituted by a genealogical *tree*
Of white Christian merchants, of lawyers, *of*
Military men, of land & slave owners penning *liberty*
(Not a true priest nor farmer, nor artist, nor *must-*
Ache among them): the laws constituted must naturally *be*
Intended to maintain, sustain & occasionally *refresh*
The power (equal to freedom) of people like them *with*
Little thought about others. Will you go to war with *the*
Appropriate weapon? Men armed with self-righteous *blood*
Will break you & laws very often. Make something *of*
Your suffering if you mean to survive it. Heroes & *patriots*
Are defined as those with a mind for sacrifice *and*
A love for country when defined by fools & *tyrants*.

# WOOLWORTH

*November 2020*

Across the street from the men in bars of booze,
Music & confinement a dog walked into a diner
To find diners eating, a cat eating, a mouse eating,
A daddy longlegs spider, & an empty stool

At the lunch counter beside a quartet of black boys
Eating nothing. The dog leapt nimbly from floor
To stool, a pair of paw-cushions barely touching
Seat cushion as it jumped from stool to the counter,

And turned its snarl directly upon the cat, who paused
In its meal of the mouse, who paused as well
In its meal of one of those daddy longlegs spiders
Folk say are extremely poisonous but whose fangs

Are too short to break anybody's skin,
Not the shorter-legged daddy longlegs arachnid
That shares its name with the spider
And secretes a small poison when attacked.

"A man walks into a bar & sets a big ugly dog bone
Down on the bar," the cat says to the snarling dog
Without clarifying whether it might be the bone of a dog
Or the bone of a man mauled by the dog.

"The man sets the bone down beside a wad of cash
And orders a tall tumbler of the most expensive whiskey
In the bar. Into which he dips the nasty tip of the bone
Stirring slowly while looking around the bar

With its stunned oblivious witnesses & big-bellied barkeep
Before quickly guzzling every drop of the burning amber,"

The cat says to the dog & an equally stunned audience
In the diner previously predisposed by the four young African-

American men who'd entered the diner to dine,
All of them now rapt & wrapped in the yarn being spun
By the cat. "When the man rose to depart, leaving the bone
Behind, the bartender snapped, 'You can't leave that lying there!'

And the man said, 'That ain't no lion, man,'" chuckled the cat.
The dog had leapt nimbly to & from the stool,
Which was one of those tall spinning stools you sometimes find
A small child set & spinning upon while the father drinks

In bars of phony euphony before stumbling from the bar
Like a dog with three legs, but this dog was not like that,
Nor was it the kind of dog you might recall turned snarling
On the black college students in Greensboro sit-ins in the sixties,

It was not a dog like that, but the dog shook its head
With the look of someone suddenly violently slapped,
And then said to the brothers who'd simply entered the diner
To dine, "Holy shit, it's a goddamned talking cat!"

# THE KAFKA VIRUS VERSES: THURSDAY

*July 2020*

The madness of each ordinary day versus
the language of someone raised by history
versus someone raised by a virgin.
I'm mostly interested in the devil's story,

because I know there's some devil in me.
I still live like someone somewhere
will clean the vents of my home anatomy,
but I am the only person who lives here.

According to Memphis Slim what looks like singing
has its roots in slaves' casting shade
on oppressors, a cotton field of them stooped weeping
jeremiads of sweat. Marlon Brando's snake-

skin jacket in *The Fugitive Kind* cursed Marlon
Brando's leather jacket in *The Wild One*
so that Brando himself became a black person
on opposite sides of a mirror calling the other Demon.

I am a man named your father's name
or I am the heroin flower vendor
vending stolen flowers in the park. I am
Ambrose Black-Blake, the Butcher,

or Ebenezer Nebuchadnezzar, the Lying King.
Or a man who thinks winning is
the whole point of everything
while losing only highlights loss.

I am known, when entangled in
great and minor trouble, to berate

my own damn self. You find every kind
of human being human in every way every day.

If you are the only person to observe
a particular trait in yourself, how trustworthy is
the observation? People who have
been loved poorly may or may not be cursed

to love poorly. You know how you don't know
how to describe your own face
without looking in the mirror? You know
how you never can tell a curse from a bad day?

That intermittent chirping coming
from somewhere in the house is a smoke
alarm's dying battery not a mine canary. Growing
is never not a part of being grown. Most

big decisions are made without me and you
every day too. I'm just so accustomed to
adjusting to everything. How often must I tell you
I was born to a sixteen-year-old black girl who

had three siblings with different fathers
in the projects of South Carolina in
1971, after a neighbor raped her?
If there is no solution,

a problem is not a real problem by
definition. When my mother's grand-
mother was alive,
she lived on the dark potions of a beautician

with a mouth full of hairpins,
and an enchanted freehand
above the minds of ladies looking
to feel more lovely beneath their lovers' hands.

Like her ambidextrous skinny silver
scissors refining and lining
the edges of her extra-fine extra
magic touch, my hands were made for beautiful things.

# WATCH YOUR HEAD

# CONTINUITY

Before getting into the cab, she hands him a cup.
Then, after they kiss, she hands him the cup again.

As they walk, she hands him a man-made substance.
Then, after they kiss, she hands him the cup again.

She hands him a chalice of lightning
And he hands her a chalice of fire.

Then, in the next shot after they kiss,
They exchange chalices again.

When she goes through the metal detector,
She carefully places a pair of hoop earrings in a plastic tray.

When she retrieves them,
They are two silver bangles she fits to her wrists.

When they climb from the cab in the rain, her hair is wet,
But when they kiss on the sidewalk, her hair is dry again.

After she takes off her helmet & breastplate,
And enters the water wearing nothing but courage,

She says to him, "You are nude,
But you must be naked to win."

But the subtitles read,
"To survive, you must bear the heart."

When they climb from the river her hair is a river
Where night has fallen, tangled with twigs & stars,

Parting like a path of escape,
But in the very next shot

As they climb from the river,
Her hair is braided with wire & string.

When he bangs on the rain-streaked window
Of the cab yelling her name in a pivotal scene,

Briefly reflected in the window in the rain
Tangled with wires & stars above a river

Is the hand of a fan or stagehand, bodyguard,
Body double, bystander, interloper, beloved ghost,

And the two of us watching from a bridge on the far side.

## AMERICAN SONNET FOR MY PAST AND FUTURE ASSASSIN

The only single women widows now or brides
Half married to the breeze. We lie to stay together.
We lie to make do. We lie to break the truth
Apart. We lie to shake fruit from the trees.
My mother favored the worker bee, her love buzzed
With stickiness & sting. I'm here about the widow
Afraid of butterflies. A widow knows ruin may be
As comprehensive as "rain," a kind of cover
For the dirt about the dead. Nature does not destroy,
Only change. Get down on your knees & pray
And get up quickly & live to celebrate that.
Falling is the first & most important skill in many things.
How to fall without breaking as well as how to break.
Tell me what you pray when you are broken or break.

## HOW TO FOLD

Seated alone at the edge of the bed,
grasp the finest fabric first,

the shrunken sock or silk softest to touch
among laundry high & hot enough

to wreathe your body in rags & towels
and undivided multicolor trappings.

When you find your phantom lover's
item in the pile, you will have to decide

how to handle it. When it is an undergarment,
you may grasp the heat

which does not linger in silk or lace.
When it is a shirt or pair of jeans, position

the fabric upon your skin in the absent
lover's position. Most of your armor is cotton.

You may undress & lie with the item
against the most exposed part of your seams,

a root work of threads like veins.
The scent folded into the fabric may no longer be

detectable to the unknowing nose.
Folded on the bed alone, conjure the lover

under some fabricated light streaming
into the room, a milk-blue ink

at some temperatures, a lucid plasma,
a pearl on the bud and palette in others.

Place your fingers as the fingers are placed.
The oblivious spirit folds out of its material.

Washed till worn, then worn despite the tatters.
Fold the legs and arms

until the figure fits neat as a book
of matches in a drawer. The map inside & out

is a mix of missteps & crossroads
bordering cliffs and edges. You cannot live

without the heat and iron of love.
The scent folded into the material travels

as far as music. The scent is like lavender
if lavender was meat-salted & emitting

a heat that travels as far as music.

# CANTO FOR GHOSTS

Every eye turned to the side door
when Frank Stanford entered
with a band called the David Bermans
& that black coiling, locking
orphan head of hair that gave him
the aura of a grizzly bear.
The Appalachian dust belly up
on the asphalt where it broke
to a gravel under the sky in a country
& western song penned by David Berman.
A "Transcript of Surreptitiously Taped
Conversations among German Nuclear
Physicists Learning America Had Dropped
an Atomic Bomb on Hiroshima" appears
on the final page of *menthol mountains*
along with Thomas Bernhard
quotes, the late Bill Knott's blog,
& a list of other David Bermans.
The boots of Johnny Paycheck were set
on the headstone & his voice came
over the air like avid static, avid whiskey,
avid hunger, avid evening, avid spirit,
avid ultraviolet colors van Gogh dreams
straitjacketed at the asylum.
David Berman dropped by the wake
disguised as Frank Stanford feigning a frank,
standoffish, storefront-philosopher pose.
A kisser chock-full of liquors
& sundowns puked along the bars
& boulevards of every Memphis
on the planet. Some roads
are illegible as the handwritten map
someone leaves for a bride while others
are illegible like the handwritten map

someone leaves for a widow.
David Berman, the plastic surgeon
who reattached John Bobbitt's
penis; David Berman, mobster
& co-owner of the Flamingo Hotel
with Bugsy Siegel. After dreaming of himself
as a young Elvis, the inverse Dylan,
the not-so-antipodal Apollinaire
out of breath in *Love Me Tender*,
where he plays a tragic Confederate,
David Berman wakes in a new goatee
styled similarly to the goatees worn
by General Grant & General Lee
at Appomattox. David Berman,
when he reappears on the doorstep
of his beloved, will be the sad king
whose queen is kidnapped by pirates
as well as the wild troubadour
who rescues her & then recounts
for the court, at great length, his exploits
with aid of his blade, his fiddle,
a keyboardist, a drummer & his horse.
The troubadour falls for the queen.
Berman steps out of a mom & pop tavern
wearing large metaphysical prescription
sunglasses & singing faintly
but poetically & thereby briefly
outflanking the ghosts oppressing
his sub-neocortex. There's a familiar tune
in the frequency of David Berman
frequenting the walkie-talkie
frequency of Stephen Malkmus
paroling the Whitney in the nineties
half appearing to be actors playing
security guards in a Jim Jarmusch
movie. David Berman, author

of *Do Good Design*, a book on ethical
standards for graphic designers;
David Berman, the theoretical physicist;
David Berman, the Irish philosopher.
Amid the overflow of fire at the campsite
of the cookout in the deep summer
alive with gnats & mosquitoes
& high devil weather bearing down
on diners gathered to hear David Berman
whistle a blues originally composed
by Tommy Johnson, the less famous
of the two bluesmen to sell
their souls for aesthetics at the crossroads.
Everyone in these parts plays or knows
someone who plays in a band
on the weekends. The strum & twang
of the Delta guitar Frank Stanford plays
in the band called the David Bermans
sings out over the eternal evening.

# BLOOD PRESSURE MEDICINE

Those instances I stayed
with my lone grandmother

moving backward
in the early morning

and that terminal quiet
between hearing her

close the door of the bathroom
and open the bathroom mirror.

My whole childhood feels
like autumn: when the multiple

browns of earth climb into leaves,
multiple points of view,

multiple labors to conjure
an imperfect painting

of the living business,
the lifeboat, the breath

machine in a rib cage,
the brain language,

the systems of currency,
the blood current,

the electricity, the spine
of the upright, downtrodden,

holy unholy rattle of wiring.
I recall the morning song

of her pills in a bottle
now that my song

is in the pills
in the bottle at hand.

# ANOTHER GREAT RAVAGER OF THE CROPS WAS THE BOLL WEEVIL

Right now, when I should be considering the tracks
Of black folk slanting in fast-drying two-dimensional colors,

I am picturing a brood of boll weevils migrating to the US
In bales of Mexican cotton or maybe in the bowels

Of the great Galveston hurricane or the ears
Of four apocalypse horses or maybe somewhere

On an oblivious industrial train traveling from one corner
Of the South to another right around the time sharecroppers

And other restless black folk decided it was time to head north.
You can probably hear me humming Lead Belly's

"Boll Weevil Blues." Sometimes an image leads you to a song.
The boll weevils Jacob Lawrence painted are little more

Than silhouettes, but a southern landowner would have
Recognized them as symbols of bad luck, bold evil:

The money eaters. The boll weevil's scientific name,
*Anthonomus grandis*, sounds like "Grand Anonymous,"

Which is as good a name as any for a force that sows trouble
Wherever it roams. "He's just a-looking for a home"

Is a common refrain in a dozen or so different boll weevil songs.
They crossed the Cotton Belt ravaging about sixty miles a year

And reached the Carolinas long before I was born,
But I wouldn't know them from the raspberry weevils,

Or apple blossom weevils, or the weevils that share
My appetite for corn. I have never talked with a boll weevil,

But when I hear crickets cricketing, I know insects
And cussing creatures like us basically ponder the same things:

Solace, survival, multiple genres of longing. I remember how
Seeing a white woman walking alone a few steps ahead of me

One night scared me so much I slowed & cast a harmless
Old song into evening. Sometimes even at a distance,

I know what unsettles my country can also unsettle me.
Sometimes fear tells us exactly where we are heading.

# THE UNDERWORLD MARVIN GAYE WALKING TOUR

On my second visit to Ostend
the Belgian shore town

Marvin Gaye lived in
in self-exile a few years

before his father killed him
I recalled my first visit & how

there was no sign Gaye had ever been there
I could not find the inn he stopped in

after dragging nothing but baggage
back from the underworld

There was no evidence he signed
the guestbook "Orpheus" in the invisible inn

I knew the route of transportable waters
I knew the river of flame blackened

or enlightened the soul
drowning or floating

but I did not know how the river of sadness
was different from the river of tears

The first time I set out
on the trail of Marvin Gaye

I was a man with no shadow
in the darkness

After midnight a loud terrible band
of tone-deaf townsfolk

played in the inn I dreamed
Gaye used to haunt

Though he could not recall
the exact song sung back then

the ancient barkeep recalled
Marvin Gaye singing a cappella

a few chilly off-season evenings
to melancholy women

who were something more
than wooed by the miraculous now

nearly forgotten sound
of what may have been for some

the only time in a lifetime
a man like him sang like that to them

# STRANGE AS THE RULES OF GRAMMAR

The two or three times I saw Lil Wayne
hanging out at the Praline Connection

in New Orleans he had a mouth full of bling
covered in forkfuls of greens or green beans

or white rice & red beans on a tongue
of strange lucrative grammar

The answer will be that which allows
the best possible future when the plaintiffs come

before the judge or the farmers
before the king it is not that which incurs unrest

The photograph does not belong
to the photographer it belongs to the camera

God jerry-rigs to the backs of a barn owl & a bat
We get a bird's-eye view via the camera

attached to the bat under cover of fur & weather
strange as the rules of grammar

Like the branch of the forest industry
tasked with trimming branches

Strange as the sound of your signature on paper
All the animals unbeknownst to us

communicate using telepathy
The owl films the room wherein

you are reflecting on something
strange as the rules of grammar

Between being grounded & being buried
between being anchored & sinking

You know how they say at the forked tongue
of the crossroads & at the crooked foot of the foothills

nothing you haven't already heard
Strange as the first wound you ever received

The scar is so old others must tell you
how it was made

# CAPRA AEGAGRUS HIRCUS

*for Ua*

No one knew the reason the town goat
followed the flower vendor around town
until someone found piles of damp petals
along the routes the flower vendor took.

All the kinfolk of the goat had long
become food. Their bones & muscles
had been used for tools & weapons.
Mannish water, a popular goat stew,

was made from the feet, intestines
& testicles of some goats. Cashmere
came from the undercoat of superfine
fibers on the underbelly of other goats.

Because the goat is one of the oldest
domesticated animals, it was one of the first
to be sacrificed in rituals, cooked in a hole
of fire, thrown off the side of a mountain.

Our goat followed the vendor around town,
dragging chains anytime there was a death
& dragging bells anytime a child was born.
The goat had no name. Or each of us called it

a different name, but when we draped its horns
in wreaths of fruit & flowers at harvesttime,
we called it *Cornucopious the Goat*. Dionysus
spent his childhood disguised as a goat

under Zeus's protection, but he went mad
when he was turned back into a human.

Goats have pupils flat as slits in their irises.
A goat is more likely to ram a man

than a ram. Our goat pooped flowers
whether we fed it meat from the table
or the butcher's block or even if it ate a rodent
at the roadside after scaring the buzzards off.

*Buzzards* because when you put an ear
to the bird, it sounded like bees in a hive.
The average goat is well known
for pinpoint balance in precarious places,

for climbing trees with hooves like ballerina
shoes & for escaping escape-proof enclosures.
When grazing undisturbed, goats maintain
social distance, but sheep huddle together.

Goats don't care for rain, rivers, or seas.
Goats converse with people about as well
as dogs & horses do. When your grandfather's
grandfather was alive, he used to say,

"I'll be here to eat the goat that eats the grass
on your grave." Many years later you were born
stubbornly side-eyeing the doctor at your delivery.
Maybe your mother had been given a magic

goat's milk by the midwife. I brought flowers
& the bells & babbling of a goat.
You spoke immediately as well as a goat.
I'm sorry I have always listened so poorly.

## AMERICAN SONNET STARRING OCTAVIA BUTLER II

In Gordon Parks's lost *Octavia Butler* photos Parks parks Butler
In Central Park & shoots her against the stars beginning to burn
Between the leaves & city some twilight evening in 1963.
She's a teen, but tall & nearly as quiet as the trees & policemen
Hovering over the scene. Parks shoots her leaning in the shade
Of the tallest tree, then clutching a hatchet at it, then transformed
Into a small black bird perched in its branches. No police dogs
Are on the attack. Rain makes the tree bark appear
To be sweating. The surface of everything cries over the black
Holes between capitalism & spirituality; the manholes between
Building & property. When asked about the banter shared
During their time together, Butler & Parks recalled different things.
If you see suffering's potential as art, is it art or suffering?
If you see life's potential as art, is it artful or artificial living?

# BOB ROSS PAINTS YOUR PORTRAIT

Today we're going to get to work on the details
of your expression. And believe it or not,
the only colors we're going to use will be

blacker than most blacks. We'll use a black canvas
& just a single finger instead of a brush.
So let's take & dab the tip of a pointer finger

in the black like so. And now we're going to touch
everything between jawbone & temple, cheek
& nostril, lip & eyebrow on both sides of the mouth.

You folks at home are welcome to use a thumb.
Use a pinkie or pinkie toe. I just want you to enjoy
yourselves. Get the feel of the color until it suits you.

And just gently tap, tap gently the color
into the shape of a forehead. There we go.
Maybe like we're looking for a tiny button to press.

We want it all to be approximately the same deep-space
black, black-hole black moving between our canvas
& fingertip. Gently, tapping, barely touching

layers of fingerprint until we have the look
of a deeply textured black. Mm-kay.
Now we're going to put some of the past

in the background around your mind
all the way out to the edges of the canvas
where all kinds of things are happening.

In the distance, maybe we'll place a mother
& father but we'll only make them visible
in your expression.

What's so very nice about these black canvases is
if there's light shining directly on them,
they look totally different.

The night sky, the landscape, the mother & father,
we want it all to disappear & appear to disappear.
It's almost like two paintings in one.

We want to touch gently enough to calm
the longing. The boundless beauty bound in you.
Like so. Mm-kay. Now we can begin applying

little black stars in the background
without changing our technique very much.
Wherever we picture stars, we can just

touch the canvas like so. We can add
black stars for eyes & black stars for scars.
We want it as black as the space around a constellation.

There we go. And maybe we want to take & add
a little bit more of the past. It's happening all the time.
Just enough to convey what we're trying to feel:

the texture beneath the finger. Mm-kay.
And maybe one parent is a little bigger
than the other in some way.

Maybe one gives you your stinger & the other
gives you your shell. So you'll have to work
a little bit harder to forgive yourself.

And just lay in some of your favorite color,
which is black, under the blackness: lamp black
& ink black, boot black & blackjack & blacker.

Just gently, tap-tap-tapping.
Now, I think I mentioned it earlier, but in case
you missed it, if you have questions or comments,

or something we can help you with, please feel free
to drop us a line. Lay in some blue black, ivory black,
jet black & blacker. Gently, tapping & touching.

There we go. I'd just love to hear from you.
You have all kinds of beautiful depths
& layers & shapes & shades of black about you.

Yes, you do. Okay, now we're going to handle your hair
like a lovely coat of black feathers, or it might be
a black feather hat, wig, afro, or aura.

We'll take our finger & just make little crosses
across your crown. Folks trying this at home,
might want to make big bold plus signs when you feel

bold & expansive. Whatever you like.
Black as hair the night before it turns gray
in the darkness, the color of sadness or escape.

(I can't shake the memory of the woman
I loved poorly curling her finger as if pointing up
inside herself when she showed me

how she wished to be touched.)
If we pick up a little bit of the darkness
under the color, that's okay. That's just fine.

We want to pull the darkness out from the edge
& blend it over the curve of your nose following
the curve of your speech down into the onyx,

the gunmetal, the black-magic-rabbit-hole
of a top hat over the mind kind of black
moving between canvas & finger. Take your time.

Soon the darkness stands back from you a little,
everything in the background where your body
begins & ends. Can you feel yourself emerge

as you fall backward? Wait till you hear
what I've got planned for next week: Is who hurt you
equal to who you hurt? Is who you love equal

to who loves you? We'll start right there & move
in the direction of desire. But right now,
let's begin working on your shadows.

## DIY SESTINA:
## WHAT WOULD YOU ASK THE ARTIST?

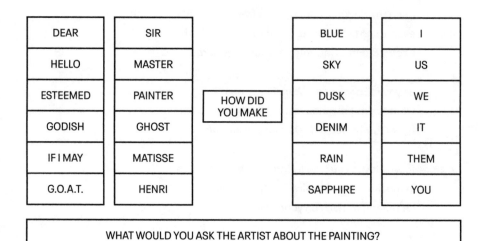

| | | | | |
|---|---|---|---|---|
| DEAR | SIR | | BLUE | I |
| HELLO | MASTER | | SKY | US |
| ESTEEMED | PAINTER | HOW DID YOU MAKE | DUSK | WE |
| GODISH | GHOST | | DENIM | IT |
| IF I MAY | MATISSE | | RAIN | THEM |
| G.O.A.T. | HENRI | | SAPPHIRE | YOU |

WHAT WOULD YOU ASK THE ARTIST ABOUT THE PAINTING?

\* \* \*

Dear Painter, can you share how you made the blue we
Find in certain of your paintings? Sometimes I catch it
Throwing a Godish glow over everything in the eye
Of a storm covered in lightning. I fear without you
The color will not be seen again except perhaps inside us
Where the bones hold its mercurial shades in them.

Matisse, sir, did your brushes have the blues in them?
Where else might the remains be found? We
Sometimes find the color in denim when rain dampens it.
Once or twice, making love, when I closed my eyes
I found myself in a tabernacle of the hue you
Have left hanging on the walls around us.

Hello, GOAT, Master of the Show, I have very little use
For blueberries, blue jays, skies, sapphire & the hems
In the garments of policemen, but the lines we
See hand-painted on porcelain come close. I might use it
On a Ming vase or in cases of chaos or rapture & if I
Fell into darkness, I would gaze upon it & thank you.

Mid-fall, Icarus shows how a misstep expands behind you,
How one can come to a conclusion using the wrong calculus.
The man who covered his coins in honey before eating them
In "Gooseberries" also turned a distasteful blue. The ennui we
Wish to cover & uncover & free & contain. As in how hard it
Is to describe your own accent. As in the way *The Bluest Eye*

Has so much Blackness in it. If people born in a season of ice
Are usually crawling by summer, how much do you
Suppose that determines their general disposition? Above us
Are constellations a soul needs for guidance, the anthems
Of sawdust & approximation. As if in matters of our bodies we
Are the least reliable witnesses. You find upon exit

The tubes of desuetude painters used in the exhibit.
I was born for this moment because this is the moment I
Was born, you say. It is always the color of history. Can you
Share how you made the blues outlast & outline us,
How long did you swim or drown or float or swallow them,
Esteemed Ghost, Henri, if I may, ennui, Henri, ennui?

\* \* \*


## ENVOY OF PICASSO'S BLUE

The first drawing Pablo Picasso made as a toddler,
With a single blue crayon on onionskin,
Made his father, an average painter, weep

And weep again showing the drawing to Picasso's mother,
Who also wept. The drawing was said to have been lost
After the death of Picasso's sister, Conchita, of diphtheria

When the family moved to Barcelona, but it
Reappeared years later somewhere you'd never expect.
To truly grasp any of Picasso's later work you should know

Whether the sister's death conjured a bird's- & bull's-
Eye view of loss & faith & if the experience
Instilled a constant mysterious feeling in him,

Whether everything that happens to the artist before
Age nine or ten or even before nine or ten a.m. influences
Whether an instrument is held like a tool or weapon.

Loss, like desire, is always in the eye
Of the maker & beholder. Picasso, of course, grew
To make many more haunted perceptive scenes,

But the stranger who found the drawing had no idea
Who'd made it, only that the lines in blue crayon
On onion paper conjured a mysterious feeling in him.

"It looks somehow like a perfectly drawn landscape,"
Said the neighbor, resting his wiry hand
On his garden fence, thinking the stranger showing him

A drawing in the middle of the day slightly stranger than
He'd thought before. Returning to his dirt when the stranger
Left, the neighbor felt something come over his eyes:

The quixotic quaking in all his blind spots
He spent the rest of his days trying to describe.
It was a depiction of the body's geometries, the eye doctor

Replied when the stranger asked his opinion. He sent
The stranger home after an inconclusive eye exam & then
Went home to bed himself. The doctor closed his eyes

Around his tears & slept for six or seven days dreaming
Of nudes posing before a surgeon with a palette knife.
When the stranger got home & showed the drawing

To his wife, she said it was clearly a portrayal of liberty.
The artist marking the presence of God, she explained,
Pausing over the thickest of the lines, "and asking why

And which heartbreaks can conjure the opposite of faith
And time." Her hair, the stranger noticed, was no longer
As it was when she was his bride. "Blind spots always leave

A stain," the wife said after dinner, though the stranger
Had long put the drawing away. She kept trying to describe
What she'd seen. "How not to disappear completely,"

She said, lying in bed while her husband, the stranger,
Saw the drawing burning in a nightmare. It was clearly a tale
About slaves. The artist was suffering a notion of color.

The wife cried herself to sleep that night & dreamed
She was being covered in waves of salt water & gold,
The ephemera of souls lost between African & American

Shores, a blue between the sky & shark parlor,
Lovely as the loveliest of the sisters to leap
Into the waters & live free as the bride of the sea.

# NOTES

The quatrains of "Watch Your Step: The Kafka Virus" were started in quarantine in April 2020 and continued through December 2020. "Do Not Put Your Head Under Your Arm," "Muscular Fantasy," and "Things Seen Right & Left Without Glasses" are titles in Erik Satie's "furniture music" composition. "Do Not Put Your Head Under Your Arm" is an analogue PechaKucha, a presentation format in which the presenter speaks about twenty slides or images for twenty seconds each.

The DIY sestinas "What Does the Piece Remind You Of?" and "What Would You Ask the Artist?" were part of three DIY sestinas to be presented at the Phillips Collection museum in Washington, DC, for the exhibit "Riffs and Relations: African American Artists and the European Modernist Tradition." When the event was canceled in April 2020 amid the COVID-19 pandemic, I sent the DIY sestina form so that those who would have been present at the event could try writing their own ekphrastic poems in quarantine.

"What Does the Piece Remind You Of?" tracks where six paintings from the collection take me. The envoy of the poem takes a longer look at a single painting by William H. Johnson, an African American painter born in my home state of South Carolina in 1901. "What Would You Ask the Artist?" explores the blues in Matisse, which naturally leads to also thinking about the blues of Picasso.

In my comments accompanying the poems, I wrote, "If we were together, and you might be coming back to your seats after twenty minutes. Maybe you'd have a little pen and paper for notes. You'd say as much as you wish. What does the piece remind you of? What question would you ask the artist? What was used to make the piece? I'd give you another twenty or thirty minutes to make your DIY sestina machines and sestina lines. We'd share."

The traditional sestina (concocted by a French troubadour in the twelfth century) is a thirty-nine-line poem that repeats six end words (teleutons) in six six-line stanzas (sestets) in an interlocking cycle, and ends with a seventh, three-line stanza (envoy that uses all six teleutons. The sestina's numerological architecture and lexical repetition create a lyrical, potentially alchemical energy. The DIY sestina works like a linguistic slot machine of multiple teleutons rotating on the gears of your input.

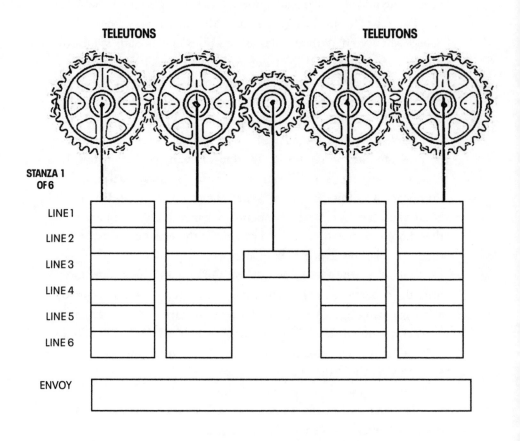

**TELEUTONS**　　　　　　　　　　　　**TELEUTONS**

STANZA 1
OF 6

LINE 1

LINE 2

LINE 3

LINE 4

LINE 5

LINE 6

ENVOY

\* \* \*

If you are unable to grasp the DIY sestina engine concept, try constructing a model using paper, ingenuity, and any additional necessary materials. Figuratively shape the materials. Carefully cut the spoke grooves. Make sure each of the five gears has a circumference of teeth with a hole at the center. Feed your words into the teeth of the engine.

# TWO DO-IT-YOURSELF SESTINA STARTERS

## 1. DIY SESTINA FOR EMMETT TILL

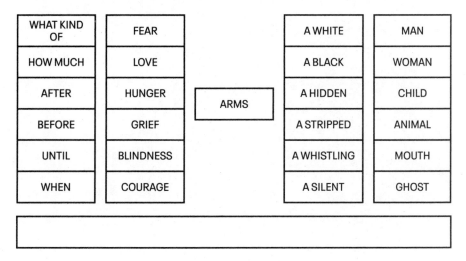

## 2. DIY SESTINA FOR THE GHOSTS WATCHING YOUR SELF

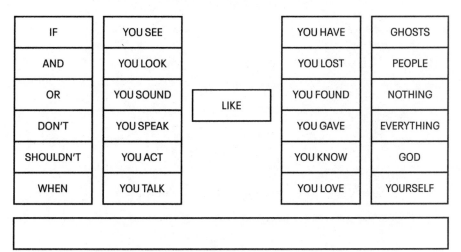

# ACKNOWLEDGMENTS

My sincere thanks to the editors and staff of the following publications for first acknowledging the poems (and previous versions of the poems) in this manuscript: Academy of American Poets *Poem-a-Day* series, *American Poetry Journal, The American Scholar, Astra Magazine, The Believer, Commonplace: The Journal of Early American Life, The Georgia Review, Harper's Magazine, The Hopkins Review, The Iowa Review, jubilat, The New Yorker, The Paris Review, Poetry, The 1619 Project: A New Origin Story, Solstice: A Magazine of Diverse Voices, The Southampton Review,* and *The Yale Review.*

"Ars Poetica with Bacon" also appeared in *The Best American Poetry 2017,* edited by Natasha Trethewey and David Lehman. "George Floyd" also appeared in *The Best American Poetry 2021,* edited by Tracy K. Smith and David Lehman. "DIY Sestina: What Would You Ask the Artist?" also appeared in *The Best American Poetry 2022,* edited by Matthew Zapruder and David Lehman. "Strange as the Rules of Grammar"("The two or three times I saw Lil Wayne") also appeared in *The Best American Poetry 2023,* edited by Elaine Equi and David Lehman. "Another Great Ravager of the Crops Was the Boll Weevil" appeared in *Jacob Lawrence: The Migration Series,* edited by Leah Dickerman and Elsa Smithgall. "Folk Stone" was originally published as "Frank Stanford as a Child of Alphabet City" in *Constant Stranger: After Frank Stanford,* edited by Aidan Matthew Ryan. "Woolworth" was reprinted in *The Madrona Project: Human Communities in Wild Places.* "George Floyd," "Do Not Put Your Head Under Your Arm," "Muscular Fantasy," "The Kafka Virus vs (Thursday)" (which first appeared as "The Kafka Verses: Thursday"), and "Things Seen Right & Left Without Glasses" were reprinted in *Life in Quarantine: Witnessing Global Pandemic* with Stanford University.

My gratitude for the support of Blue Flower Arts, New York University, and the John D. and Catherine T. MacArthur Foundation. Special gratitude to my editor, Paul Slovak, for more than twenty years of faith and support. I am indebted to Miriam Berkley, whose photograph of Octavia Butler influenced my drawing of Butler in "Illustrated Octavia Butler Do-It-Your-Self Sestina." Thanks as well to writers and artists who influenced this manuscript through encouragement and conversation: Elizabeth Alexander, Radiclani Clytus, Toi Derricotte, Joel Dias-Porter, Peter Kahn, Mary Karr, Nick Laird, Shara McCallum, Jeffrey McDaniel, Roger Reeves, and Joan Wasser. My gratitude to all who speak poetry to me.

"George Floyd" is for brothers and *bothers*. "An Extended Public Service Announcement" is for Radiclani Clytus, Alisha Sett, and South Carolina. "Maps of States" is for Solomon "Solo" Alexander's May 2020 college graduation. "Canto for Ghosts" is for David Berman (1967–2019). "Pseudacris Crucifer" is for my son. "Capra Aegagrus Hircus" is for my daughter.

**Terrance Hayes** is the author of *American Sonnets for My Past and Future Assassin*, winner of the 2019 Hurston/Wright Legacy Award, and *Lighthead*, winner of the 2010 National Book Award. His other poetry collections are *How to Be Drawn, Wind in a Box, Hip Logic*, and *Muscular Music*. He is also the author of *Watch Your Language: Visual and Literary Reflections on a Century of American Poetry* and *To Float in the Space Between: A Life and Work in Conversation with the Life and Work of Etheridge Knight*, winner of the 2019 Poetry Foundation Pegasus Award for Poetry Criticism. His honors include a National Endowment for the Arts Fellowship, a Guggenheim Fellowship, and a 2014 MacArthur Fellowship. Hayes lives in New York City, where he is a professor of creative writing at New York University.

# PENGUIN POETS

# PENGUIN POETS